Yummy Fruit
of the Spirit

To request permission, contact the author at CieraSpeaksLife@gmail.com

Hardcover ISBN: 979-8-88759-761-4
Paperback ISBN: 979-8-88759-743-0
E-book ISBN: 979-8-88759-744-7

Editor: Shalonda Wallace
Cover Designer: Jeanly Zamora and Maria Musaddaq
Illustrators: Ciera Speaks, Maria Musaddaq, and Anosha Chaand

Special Contributors: Amari, Amir, and Bobby Jennings
                       Endia Chapman and Holly Arceneaux

Yummy Fruit
of the Spirit

Ciera Speaks

Do you like yummy fruits?

What's your favorite fruit to eat?

Some fruits grow low on the ground.
Some fruits grow high in the trees.

Apple
Trees

Melon

Watermelon Patch

Mangoes

Orange Tree

Fruits are healthy and good for you.
Most of them are sweet and colorful.

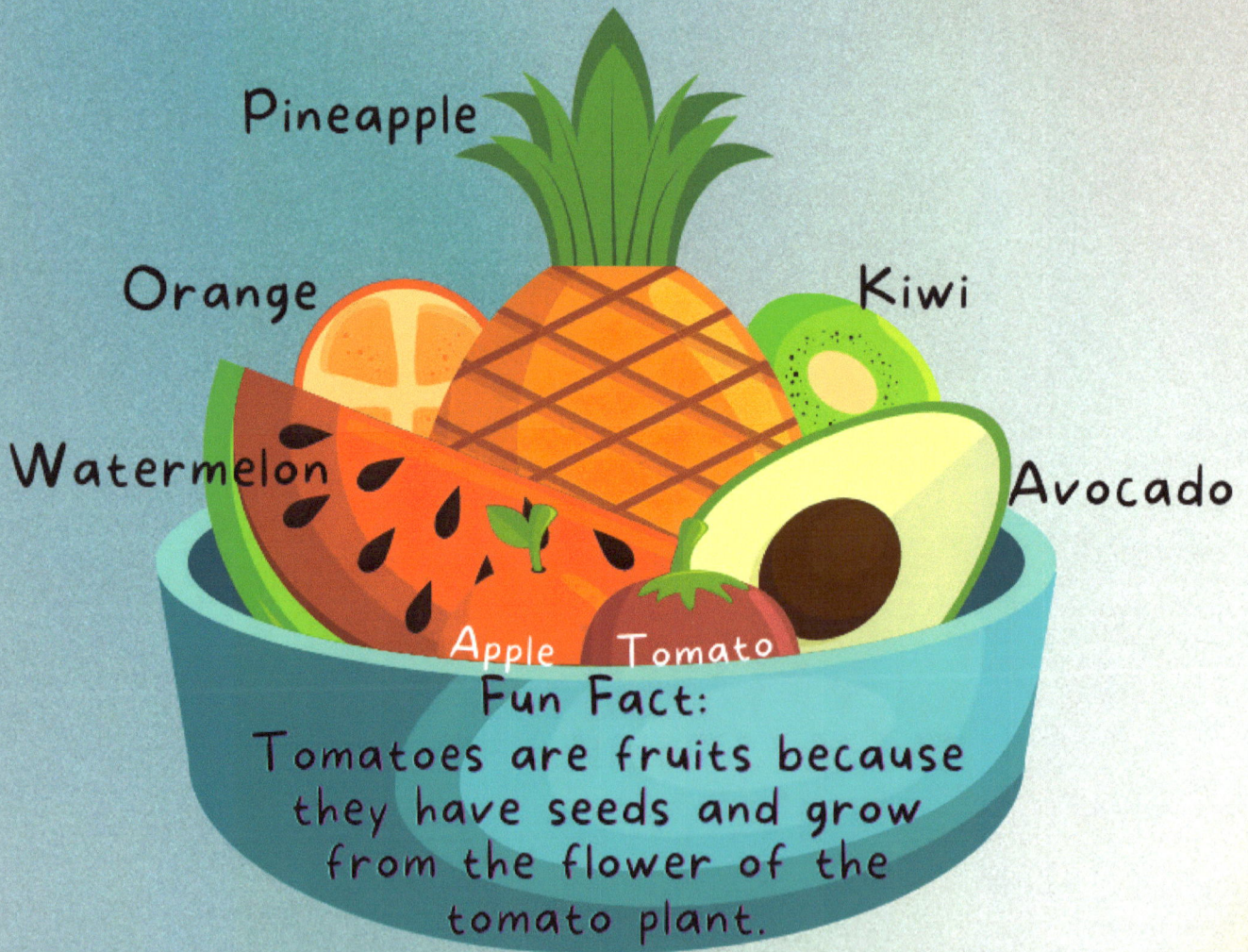

Pineapple

Orange

Kiwi

Watermelon

Avocado

Apple   Tomato

Fun Fact:
Tomatoes are fruits because
they have seeds and grow
from the flower of the
tomato plant.

Berries, cherries, plums, and pears... an abundance of fruits everywhere!

Plum

Grapes

Blueberries

Pear

Bananas

Apricot

Cherries

Strawberry

There is another type of fruit
from the Creator above.
Fruit that tells people all about who you are.
This kind of fruit is always fresh.
The Fruit of the Spirit is the very best.

The Fruit of the Spirit is not
something you eat.
It does not grow from the ground
or up in the trees.

It is an invisible fruit that grows inside everyone who strives to live right.

"What is this mystery fruit?"
You may be wondering now.

Today, we will learn all about how it makes the world go around.

Galatians 5:22-23

The Fruit of the Spirit is love, joy, peace, patience, kindness, goodness, faithfulness, gentleness, and self-control.

To have the fruit of love means to show that you care. Treat yourself and others with respect and always be fair.

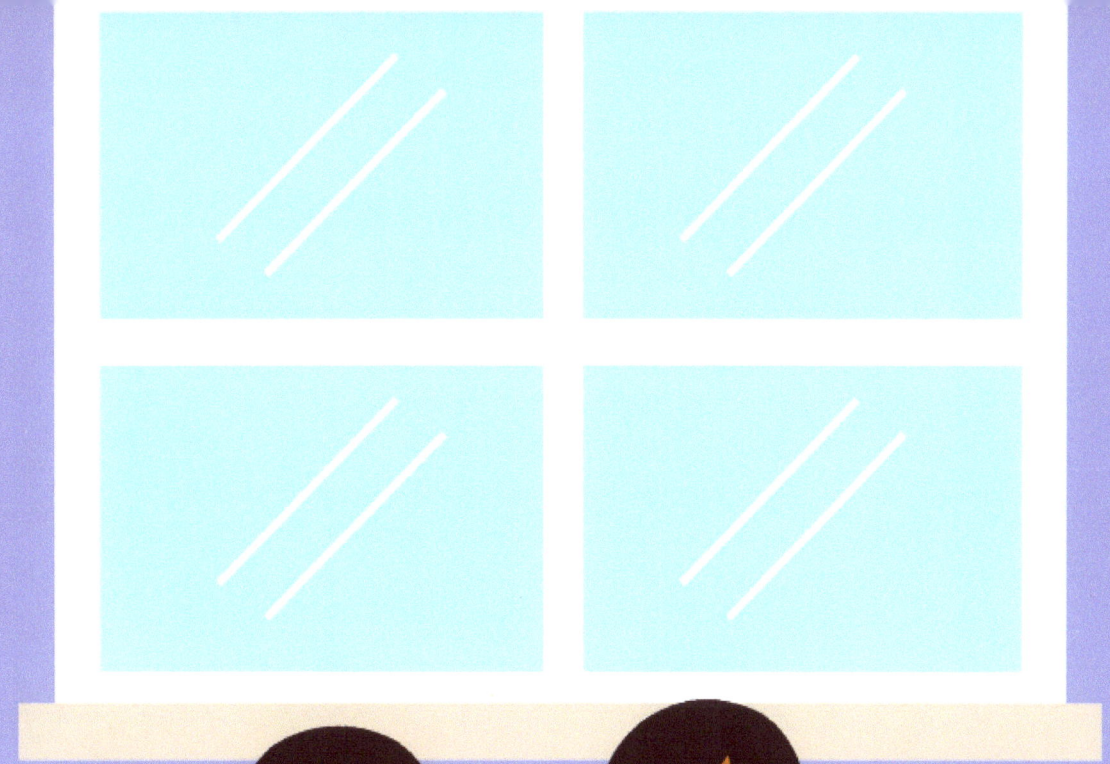

Love is patient, love is kind. (I Corinthians 13:4)

To have the fruit of joy means to be grateful for life no matter what...

Dance,
Laugh,
Play,
Rejoice!

whether things are going great
or whether things are tough.

To have the fruit of peace means
to be calm during a storm.
Trust that God is near and within
you, no matter what is going on.

The Most High
is our refuge
and strength.
(Psalm 46:1)

To have the fruit of patience means
To kindly wait your turn.

Welcome to school

To have the fruit of kindness means
to be helpful and show concern.

To have the fruit of goodness means to let your light shine. Share with your friends and think good thoughts in your mind.

To have the fruit of faithfulness
means to believe in the Most High,
who is always reliable and right on time.

Don't worry about anything,
instead pray about everything.
(Philippians 4:6)

To have the fruit of gentleness means to use your power and strength in loving ways.

Be careful with those not as strong as you and with those who may be having a sad day.

To have the fruit of self-control means to not overeat.

Blessed are those who hunger and thirst for righteousness, for they will be filled. (Matthew 5:6)

When you are angry be mindful of what you speak.

The Fruit of the Spirit gives you spiritual wealth,
like the fruits that you eat give
you physical health.
Both types are important and will
help you to live an awesome life!

Now that you know about the Fruit of the Spirit, which one did you share with the world today?

Which one will you share tomorrow?

Meet the Author

Hi, my name is Ciera Speaks. I'm a poet, songwriter, and jewelry designer. I enjoy going on nature walks, doing arts and crafts with my kids, and having fun with my family. I was inspired to write this book to create a simple way for children to learn about the nine fruits of the Spirit mentioned in Galatians **5:22-23** and how to share them with the world. A person is never too young to learn about the importance of the fruits that we eat as well as the fruits that we cannot eat but can certainly feel and show.

I hope you enjoy this book with every read and discover something new!

www.ingramcontent.com/pod-product-compliance
Lightning Source LLC
Chambersburg PA
CBHW041548040426
42447CB00002B/92